50 Decadent Chocolate Cake Layer Recipes

By: Kelly Johnson

Table of Contents

- Classic Chocolate Fudge Cake
- Dark Chocolate Ganache Cake
- Chocolate and Peanut Butter Layer Cake
- Mocha Chocolate Cake
- Double Chocolate Truffle Cake
- Chocolate and Raspberry Cake
- Chocolate Hazelnut Cake
- Chocolate Mint Layer Cake
- Flourless Chocolate Cake
- Chocolate Coconut Cream Cake
- Chocolate Caramel Swirl Cake
- Chocolate and Cherry Cake
- Triple Chocolate Mousse Cake
- Chocolate Chip Cookie Dough Cake
- Chocolate and Coffee Layer Cake
- Chocolate Espresso Cake
- Chocolate Almond Cake
- Chocolate Stout Cake
- Chocolate Orange Truffle Cake
- Chocolate and Salted Caramel Cake
- Chocolate and Marshmallow Layer Cake
- Chocolate and Mint Buttercream Cake
- Chocolate Velvet Cake
- Chocolate and Raspberry Cheesecake Cake
- Chocolate Coconut Meringue Cake
- Chocolate Peanut Butter Cup Cake
- Black Forest Chocolate Cake
- Chocolate Banana Layer Cake
- Chocolate Cherry Almond Cake
- Chocolate and Hazelnut Praline Cake
- Chocolate Pumpkin Spice Cake
- Chocolate Tiramisu Layer Cake
- Chocolate Lemon Layer Cake
- Chocolate Mocha Ganache Cake
- Chocolate and Macadamia Nut Cake

- Chocolate Toffee Cake
- Chocolate Almond Joy Cake
- Chocolate Cream Puff Cake
- Chocolate and Red Velvet Cake
- Chocolate Strawberry Shortcake Cake
- Chocolate and Dulce de Leche Cake
- Chocolate Fudge and Pecan Cake
- Chocolate and Bourbon Layer Cake
- Chocolate and Coconut Custard Cake
- Chocolate Blueberry Truffle Cake
- Chocolate Pistachio Cake
- Chocolate Sour Cherry Cake
- Chocolate Marshmallow Fluff Cake
- Chocolate Hazelnut Mousse Cake
- Chocolate-Covered Cherry Cake

Classic Chocolate Fudge Cake

Ingredients

For the Cake:

- 2 cups (250g) all-purpose flour
- 1 ½ tsp baking powder
- ½ tsp baking soda
- ½ tsp salt
- 1 cup (230g) unsalted butter, softened
- 1 ½ cups (300g) granulated sugar
- 3 large eggs
- 1 tsp vanilla extract
- ¾ cup (180ml) whole milk
- ¾ cup (180ml) hot water
- 6 oz (170g) semi-sweet chocolate, melted

For the Frosting:

- 1 ½ cups (360ml) heavy cream
- 8 oz (225g) semi-sweet chocolate, chopped
- 2 tbsp unsalted butter

Instructions

1. **Prepare the Cake:**
    - Preheat the oven to 350°F (175°C). Grease and line two 9-inch (23cm) round cake pans.
    - In a bowl, whisk together flour, baking powder, baking soda, and salt.
    - In a large bowl, beat the butter and sugar until light and fluffy. Add eggs one at a time, mixing well. Stir in vanilla extract and melted chocolate.
    - Gradually add the dry ingredients alternating with milk, mixing until smooth. Add the hot water and mix until combined.
    - Divide the batter between the pans and bake for 25-30 minutes or until a toothpick comes out clean. Let the cakes cool completely.
2. **Prepare the Frosting:**
    - Heat the heavy cream in a saucepan until it just begins to boil. Pour over chopped chocolate in a bowl and stir until smooth. Add butter and stir until fully incorporated.

- Let the ganache cool to room temperature, then refrigerate for 30 minutes to thicken.
3. **Assemble the Cake:**
    - Frost the cooled cakes with chocolate ganache. Decorate with chocolate shavings if desired.

Dark Chocolate Ganache Cake

Ingredients

For the Cake:

- 2 ½ cups (315g) all-purpose flour
- 1 ½ tsp baking powder
- ¼ tsp baking soda
- ½ tsp salt
- 1 cup (230g) unsalted butter, softened
- 1 ½ cups (300g) granulated sugar
- 3 large eggs
- 1 tsp vanilla extract
- 1 cup (240ml) buttermilk
- 8 oz (225g) dark chocolate, melted

For the Ganache:

- 12 oz (340g) dark chocolate, chopped
- 1 ½ cups (360ml) heavy cream

Instructions

1. **Prepare the Cake:**
   - Preheat the oven to 350°F (175°C). Grease and line two 9-inch (23cm) round cake pans.
   - In a bowl, whisk together flour, baking powder, baking soda, and salt.
   - In a large bowl, beat the butter and sugar until light and fluffy. Add eggs one at a time, mixing well. Stir in vanilla extract and melted dark chocolate.
   - Gradually add the dry ingredients alternating with buttermilk, mixing until smooth.
   - Divide the batter between the pans and bake for 25-30 minutes or until a toothpick comes out clean. Let the cakes cool completely.
2. **Prepare the Ganache:**
   - Heat the heavy cream in a saucepan until it just begins to boil. Pour over chopped dark chocolate in a bowl and stir until smooth. Allow the ganache to cool to room temperature.
3. **Assemble the Cake:**
   - Frost the cooled cakes with dark chocolate ganache. Optionally, drizzle with extra ganache for a decorative effect.

Chocolate and Peanut Butter Layer Cake

Ingredients

For the Cake:

- 2 cups (250g) all-purpose flour
- 1 ½ tsp baking powder
- ½ tsp baking soda
- ½ tsp salt
- 1 cup (230g) unsalted butter, softened
- 1 ½ cups (300g) granulated sugar
- 3 large eggs
- 1 tsp vanilla extract
- ¾ cup (180ml) whole milk
- ¾ cup (180ml) creamy peanut butter
- 1 cup (120g) cocoa powder

For the Peanut Butter Frosting:

- 1 cup (230g) creamy peanut butter
- 1 ½ cups (360g) powdered sugar
- 4 oz (115g) unsalted butter, softened
- 2 tbsp milk
- 1 tsp vanilla extract

For the Chocolate Ganache:

- 6 oz (170g) semi-sweet chocolate, chopped
- ¾ cup (180ml) heavy cream

Instructions

1. **Prepare the Cake:**
   - Preheat the oven to 350°F (175°C). Grease and line two 9-inch (23cm) round cake pans.
   - In a bowl, whisk together flour, baking powder, baking soda, salt, and cocoa powder.
   - In a large bowl, beat the butter and sugar until light and fluffy. Add eggs one at a time, mixing well. Stir in vanilla extract and peanut butter.

- Gradually add the dry ingredients alternating with milk, mixing until smooth.
- Divide the batter between the pans and bake for 25-30 minutes or until a toothpick comes out clean. Let the cakes cool completely.

2. **Prepare the Peanut Butter Frosting:**
   - Beat together peanut butter, powdered sugar, butter, milk, and vanilla extract until smooth and fluffy.
3. **Prepare the Chocolate Ganache:**
   - Heat the heavy cream in a saucepan until it just begins to boil. Pour over chopped chocolate and stir until smooth.
4. **Assemble the Cake:**
   - Frost the cooled cakes with peanut butter frosting. Drizzle the top with chocolate ganache. Optionally, garnish with crushed peanuts or chocolate chips.

Mocha Chocolate Cake

Ingredients

For the Cake:

- 2 cups (250g) all-purpose flour
- 1 ½ tsp baking powder
- ¼ tsp baking soda
- ½ tsp salt
- 1 cup (230g) unsalted butter, softened
- 1 ½ cups (300g) granulated sugar
- 3 large eggs
- 1 tsp vanilla extract
- 1 cup (240ml) coffee, brewed strong and cooled
- ½ cup (45g) cocoa powder

For the Frosting:

- 1 ½ cups (360ml) heavy cream
- 8 oz (225g) semi-sweet chocolate, chopped
- 1 tbsp instant coffee granules

Instructions

1. **Prepare the Cake:**
    - Preheat the oven to 350°F (175°C). Grease and line two 9-inch (23cm) round cake pans.
    - In a bowl, whisk together flour, baking powder, baking soda, salt, and cocoa powder.
    - In a large bowl, beat the butter and sugar until light and fluffy. Add eggs one at a time, mixing well. Stir in vanilla extract and cooled coffee.
    - Gradually add the dry ingredients, mixing until smooth.
    - Divide the batter between the pans and bake for 25-30 minutes or until a toothpick comes out clean. Let the cakes cool completely.
2. **Prepare the Frosting:**
    - Heat the heavy cream in a saucepan until it just begins to boil. Add coffee granules and stir to dissolve. Pour over chopped chocolate and stir until smooth. Let it cool to room temperature.
3. **Assemble the Cake:**
    - Frost the cooled cakes with mocha chocolate frosting.

Double Chocolate Truffle Cake

Ingredients

For the Cake:

- 2 ½ cups (315g) all-purpose flour
- 1 ½ tsp baking powder
- ¼ tsp baking soda
- ½ tsp salt
- 1 cup (230g) unsalted butter, softened
- 2 cups (400g) granulated sugar
- 3 large eggs
- 1 tsp vanilla extract
- 1 cup (240ml) whole milk
- 6 oz (170g) dark chocolate, melted
- 1 cup (120g) cocoa powder

For the Truffle Filling:

- 8 oz (225g) semi-sweet chocolate, chopped
- ¾ cup (180ml) heavy cream
- 1 tbsp unsalted butter

Instructions

1. **Prepare the Cake:**
    - Preheat the oven to 350°F (175°C). Grease and line two 9-inch (23cm) round cake pans.
    - In a bowl, whisk together flour, baking powder, baking soda, salt, and cocoa powder.
    - In a large bowl, beat the butter and sugar until light and fluffy. Add eggs one at a time, mixing well. Stir in vanilla extract and melted chocolate.
    - Gradually add the dry ingredients alternating with milk, mixing until smooth.
    - Divide the batter between the pans and bake for 25-30 minutes or until a toothpick comes out clean. Let the cakes cool completely.
2. **Prepare the Truffle Filling:**
    - Heat the heavy cream in a saucepan until it just begins to boil. Pour over chopped chocolate and stir until smooth. Stir in butter and mix until glossy. Let cool.

3. **Assemble the Cake:**
    - Once the cakes are cooled, layer them with chocolate truffle filling between each layer. Frost the top with the remaining truffle filling.

Flourless Chocolate Cake

Ingredients

For the Cake:

- 8 oz (225g) semi-sweet chocolate, chopped
- ½ cup (115g) unsalted butter
- ¾ cup (150g) granulated sugar
- 4 large eggs
- 1 tsp vanilla extract
- ¼ tsp salt

For the Ganache (Optional):

- 4 oz (115g) semi-sweet chocolate, chopped
- ¼ cup (60ml) heavy cream

Instructions

1. **Prepare the Cake:**
    - Preheat the oven to 350°F (175°C). Grease and line a 9-inch (23cm) round cake pan with parchment paper.
    - Melt the chocolate and butter together in a heatproof bowl over simmering water or in the microwave, stirring until smooth.
    - Beat the sugar, eggs, vanilla extract, and salt together in a separate bowl until thick and pale.
    - Stir in the melted chocolate mixture and mix until well combined.
    - Pour the batter into the prepared pan and bake for 20-25 minutes or until the center is set but slightly wobbly.
    - Allow the cake to cool in the pan before transferring to a wire rack.
2. **Prepare the Ganache (Optional):**
    - Heat the heavy cream in a saucepan until it begins to boil. Pour it over the chopped chocolate and stir until smooth.
    - Let the ganache cool slightly before pouring it over the cooled cake.

Chocolate Coconut Cream Cake

Ingredients

For the Cake:

- 2 cups (250g) all-purpose flour
- 1 ½ tsp baking powder
- ½ tsp baking soda
- ½ tsp salt
- 1 cup (230g) unsalted butter, softened
- 1 ½ cups (300g) granulated sugar
- 3 large eggs
- 1 tsp vanilla extract
- 1 cup (240ml) buttermilk
- 1 ½ cups (120g) shredded coconut

For the Coconut Cream Filling:

- 1 ½ cups (360ml) heavy cream
- 1 cup (120g) shredded coconut
- ½ cup (100g) powdered sugar
- 1 tsp vanilla extract

For the Chocolate Ganache:

- 8 oz (225g) semi-sweet chocolate, chopped
- ¾ cup (180ml) heavy cream

Instructions

1. **Prepare the Cake:**
    - Preheat the oven to 350°F (175°C). Grease and line two 9-inch (23cm) round cake pans.
    - In a bowl, whisk together the flour, baking powder, baking soda, and salt.
    - In a large bowl, beat the butter and sugar until light and fluffy. Add eggs one at a time, mixing well. Stir in vanilla extract.
    - Gradually add the dry ingredients alternating with buttermilk. Fold in the shredded coconut.
    - Divide the batter between the pans and bake for 25-30 minutes or until a toothpick comes out clean. Let the cakes cool completely.

2. **Prepare the Coconut Cream Filling:**
   - Whisk together heavy cream, powdered sugar, and vanilla extract in a bowl. Fold in shredded coconut until combined.
   - Refrigerate until ready to use.
3. **Prepare the Chocolate Ganache:**
   - Heat the heavy cream in a saucepan until it just begins to boil. Pour it over chopped chocolate and stir until smooth.
4. **Assemble the Cake:**
   - Frost the cooled cakes with coconut cream filling. Drizzle with chocolate ganache before serving.

Chocolate Caramel Swirl Cake

Ingredients

For the Cake:

- 2 cups (250g) all-purpose flour
- 1 ½ tsp baking powder
- ½ tsp baking soda
- ½ tsp salt
- 1 cup (230g) unsalted butter, softened
- 1 ½ cups (300g) granulated sugar
- 3 large eggs
- 1 tsp vanilla extract
- 1 cup (240ml) milk
- ¼ cup (60ml) caramel sauce

For the Caramel Frosting:

- 1 cup (230g) unsalted butter, softened
- 1 ½ cups (180g) powdered sugar
- ¼ cup (60ml) caramel sauce
- 1 tbsp milk

For the Chocolate Ganache:

- 6 oz (170g) semi-sweet chocolate, chopped
- ¾ cup (180ml) heavy cream

Instructions

1. **Prepare the Cake:**
   - Preheat the oven to 350°F (175°C). Grease and line two 9-inch (23cm) round cake pans.
   - In a bowl, whisk together the flour, baking powder, baking soda, and salt.
   - In a large bowl, beat the butter and sugar until light and fluffy. Add eggs one at a time, mixing well. Stir in vanilla extract.
   - Gradually add the dry ingredients alternating with milk. Add caramel sauce and mix until combined.
   - Divide the batter between the pans and bake for 25-30 minutes or until a toothpick comes out clean. Let the cakes cool completely.

2. **Prepare the Caramel Frosting:**
   - Beat together butter, powdered sugar, caramel sauce, and milk until smooth.
3. **Prepare the Chocolate Ganache:**
   - Heat the heavy cream in a saucepan until it just begins to boil. Pour it over chopped chocolate and stir until smooth.
4. **Assemble the Cake:**
   - Frost the cooled cakes with caramel frosting. Drizzle with chocolate ganache and swirl for a marbled effect.

Chocolate and Cherry Cake

Ingredients

For the Cake:

- 2 cups (250g) all-purpose flour
- 1 ½ tsp baking powder
- ½ tsp baking soda
- ½ tsp salt
- 1 cup (230g) unsalted butter, softened
- 1 ½ cups (300g) granulated sugar
- 3 large eggs
- 1 tsp vanilla extract
- 1 cup (240ml) buttermilk
- 1 cup (150g) fresh or jarred cherries, pitted and chopped

For the Frosting:

- 1 ½ cups (360ml) heavy cream
- 8 oz (225g) semi-sweet chocolate, chopped
- 1 tsp cherry extract (optional)

Instructions

1. **Prepare the Cake:**
    - Preheat the oven to 350°F (175°C). Grease and line two 9-inch (23cm) round cake pans.
    - In a bowl, whisk together the flour, baking powder, baking soda, and salt.
    - In a large bowl, beat the butter and sugar until light and fluffy. Add eggs one at a time, mixing well. Stir in vanilla extract.
    - Gradually add the dry ingredients alternating with buttermilk. Gently fold in the chopped cherries.
    - Divide the batter between the pans and bake for 25-30 minutes or until a toothpick comes out clean. Let the cakes cool completely.
2. **Prepare the Frosting:**
    - Heat the heavy cream in a saucepan until it just begins to boil. Pour it over chopped chocolate and stir until smooth. Optionally, stir in cherry extract for a stronger cherry flavor.
    - Allow the ganache to cool slightly before frosting the cake.
3. **Assemble the Cake:**

- Frost the cooled cakes with the chocolate ganache. Garnish with additional cherries if desired.

Chocolate Stout Cake

Ingredients

For the Cake:

- 1 cup (240ml) stout beer (such as Guinness)
- ½ cup (115g) unsalted butter
- 1 cup (200g) granulated sugar
- ½ cup (120g) sour cream
- 2 large eggs
- 1 tsp vanilla extract
- 1 ¾ cups (220g) all-purpose flour
- ¾ cup (60g) unsweetened cocoa powder
- 1 ½ tsp baking powder
- 1 ½ tsp baking soda
- ¼ tsp salt

For the Frosting:

- 8 oz (225g) cream cheese, softened
- ½ cup (115g) unsalted butter, softened
- 2 cups (240g) powdered sugar
- 1 tsp vanilla extract
- 2 tbsp stout beer (optional)

Instructions

1. **Prepare the Cake:**
    - Preheat the oven to 350°F (175°C). Grease and line two 9-inch (23cm) round cake pans.
    - In a saucepan, melt butter and stout beer together. Remove from heat and stir in the sugar, sour cream, eggs, and vanilla.
    - In a separate bowl, whisk the flour, cocoa powder, baking powder, baking soda, and salt.
    - Gradually add the dry ingredients to the wet ingredients, mixing until smooth.
    - Divide the batter between the pans and bake for 30-35 minutes or until a toothpick comes out clean. Allow the cakes to cool completely.
2. **Prepare the Frosting:**

- Beat the cream cheese and butter until creamy. Gradually add the powdered sugar and vanilla, then beat until smooth. Add stout beer if desired for extra flavor.
3. **Assemble the Cake:**
    - Frost the cooled cakes with the cream cheese frosting.

Chocolate Orange Truffle Cake

Ingredients

For the Cake:

- 1 ½ cups (190g) all-purpose flour
- 1 cup (200g) granulated sugar
- 1 tsp baking powder
- 1 tsp baking soda
- ½ tsp salt
- ½ cup (120ml) orange juice
- ½ cup (115g) unsalted butter, softened
- 2 large eggs
- 1 tsp vanilla extract
- 1 tbsp orange zest

For the Ganache:

- 8 oz (225g) semi-sweet chocolate, chopped
- ½ cup (120ml) heavy cream
- 1 tsp orange extract (or zest of 1 orange)

Instructions

1. **Prepare the Cake:**
    - Preheat the oven to 350°F (175°C). Grease and line two 9-inch (23cm) round cake pans.
    - In a bowl, whisk together flour, sugar, baking powder, baking soda, and salt.
    - In a separate bowl, combine orange juice, butter, eggs, vanilla, and orange zest. Add to the dry ingredients and mix until smooth.
    - Divide the batter between the pans and bake for 25-30 minutes or until a toothpick comes out clean. Allow the cakes to cool completely.
2. **Prepare the Ganache:**
    - Heat the heavy cream in a saucepan until it just begins to boil. Pour it over chopped chocolate and stir until smooth. Stir in the orange extract or zest.
3. **Assemble the Cake:**
    - Frost the cooled cakes with the chocolate ganache and drizzle extra ganache over the top.

Chocolate and Salted Caramel Cake

Ingredients

For the Cake:

- 2 cups (250g) all-purpose flour
- 1 ½ tsp baking powder
- ½ tsp baking soda
- ½ tsp salt
- 1 cup (230g) unsalted butter, softened
- 1 ½ cups (300g) granulated sugar
- 3 large eggs
- 1 tsp vanilla extract
- 1 cup (240ml) milk
- ¼ cup (60ml) caramel sauce
- 1 tsp sea salt

For the Salted Caramel Frosting:

- 1 cup (230g) unsalted butter, softened
- 2 cups (240g) powdered sugar
- ¼ cup (60ml) caramel sauce
- 1 tsp vanilla extract
- ½ tsp sea salt

For the Chocolate Ganache:

- 6 oz (170g) semi-sweet chocolate, chopped
- ¾ cup (180ml) heavy cream

Instructions

1. **Prepare the Cake:**
    - Preheat the oven to 350°F (175°C). Grease and line two 9-inch (23cm) round cake pans.
    - In a bowl, whisk together flour, baking powder, baking soda, and salt.
    - In a separate bowl, beat together butter and sugar until fluffy. Add eggs one at a time, mixing well. Stir in vanilla extract.
    - Gradually add the dry ingredients alternating with milk. Stir in caramel sauce and sea salt.

- Divide the batter between the pans and bake for 25-30 minutes or until a toothpick comes out clean. Allow the cakes to cool completely.
2. **Prepare the Salted Caramel Frosting:**
    - Beat together butter, powdered sugar, caramel sauce, vanilla extract, and sea salt until smooth.
3. **Prepare the Chocolate Ganache:**
    - Heat the heavy cream in a saucepan until it just begins to boil. Pour it over chopped chocolate and stir until smooth.
4. **Assemble the Cake:**
    - Frost the cakes with salted caramel frosting, drizzle with chocolate ganache, and sprinkle with sea salt.

Chocolate and Marshmallow Layer Cake

Ingredients

For the Cake:

- 2 cups (250g) all-purpose flour
- 1 ½ tsp baking powder
- 1 tsp cocoa powder
- 1 cup (230g) unsalted butter, softened
- 1 ½ cups (300g) granulated sugar
- 4 large eggs
- 1 tsp vanilla extract
- 1 cup (240ml) buttermilk

For the Marshmallow Frosting:

- 2 cups (200g) powdered sugar
- ½ cup (115g) unsalted butter, softened
- 7 oz (200g) marshmallow fluff
- 1 tsp vanilla extract

Instructions

1. **Prepare the Cake:**
    - Preheat the oven to 350°F (175°C). Grease and line two 9-inch (23cm) round cake pans.
    - In a bowl, whisk together flour, baking powder, and cocoa powder.
    - In a separate bowl, beat butter and sugar until fluffy. Add eggs one at a time, mixing well. Stir in vanilla extract.
    - Gradually add the dry ingredients alternating with buttermilk. Mix until smooth.
    - Divide the batter between the pans and bake for 25-30 minutes or until a toothpick comes out clean. Allow the cakes to cool completely.
2. **Prepare the Marshmallow Frosting:**
    - Beat together powdered sugar, butter, marshmallow fluff, and vanilla extract until smooth.
3. **Assemble the Cake:**
    - Frost the cooled cakes with marshmallow frosting.

Chocolate Peanut Butter Cup Cake

Ingredients

For the Cake:

- 1 ¾ cups (220g) all-purpose flour
- 1 ½ tsp baking powder
- 1 tsp baking soda
- ½ tsp salt
- 1 cup (240ml) milk
- ½ cup (120ml) vegetable oil
- 2 large eggs
- 1 tsp vanilla extract
- ½ cup (120g) peanut butter
- 1 cup (200g) granulated sugar
- ¼ cup (60ml) boiling water
- ½ cup (100g) semi-sweet chocolate chips

For the Peanut Butter Frosting:

- 1 cup (230g) unsalted butter, softened
- 1 ½ cups (180g) powdered sugar
- 1 cup (250g) peanut butter
- 1 tsp vanilla extract
- 2 tbsp milk (or as needed for consistency)

For the Chocolate Ganache:

- 6 oz (170g) semi-sweet chocolate, chopped
- ½ cup (120ml) heavy cream

Instructions

1. **Prepare the Cake:**
    - Preheat the oven to 350°F (175°C). Grease and line two 9-inch (23cm) round cake pans.
    - In a bowl, whisk together flour, baking powder, baking soda, and salt.
    - In a separate bowl, mix together milk, vegetable oil, eggs, vanilla, peanut butter, and sugar until well combined.
    - Gradually add the dry ingredients to the wet mixture, mixing until smooth.

- Stir in the boiling water until the batter is thin. Fold in chocolate chips.
- Divide the batter between the pans and bake for 30-35 minutes or until a toothpick comes out clean. Allow to cool completely.

2. **Prepare the Peanut Butter Frosting:**
   - Beat the butter and powdered sugar until fluffy. Add peanut butter, vanilla, and milk, mixing until smooth and creamy.
3. **Prepare the Chocolate Ganache:**
   - Heat the heavy cream in a saucepan until it just begins to boil. Pour it over chopped chocolate and stir until smooth.
4. **Assemble the Cake:**
   - Frost the cakes with peanut butter frosting. Drizzle with chocolate ganache.

Black Forest Chocolate Cake

Ingredients

For the Cake:

- 2 cups (250g) all-purpose flour
- 1 ½ tsp baking powder
- 1 tsp baking soda
- 1 tsp cocoa powder
- ½ tsp salt
- 1 cup (240ml) buttermilk
- ½ cup (120g) unsalted butter, softened
- 1 ½ cups (300g) granulated sugar
- 2 large eggs
- 1 tsp vanilla extract
- ¾ cup (180ml) maraschino cherry juice

For the Frosting:

- 2 cups (480ml) heavy cream
- 2 tbsp powdered sugar
- 1 tsp vanilla extract

For the Filling:

- 1 jar (12 oz/340g) maraschino cherries, drained
- ½ cup (120ml) cherry juice
- ½ cup (100g) semi-sweet chocolate shavings

Instructions

1. **Prepare the Cake:**
    - Preheat the oven to 350°F (175°C). Grease and line two 9-inch (23cm) round cake pans.
    - In a bowl, whisk together flour, baking powder, baking soda, cocoa powder, and salt.
    - In a separate bowl, beat together buttermilk, butter, sugar, eggs, vanilla, and cherry juice.
    - Gradually add the dry ingredients to the wet ingredients and mix until smooth.

- Divide the batter between the pans and bake for 25-30 minutes, or until a toothpick comes out clean. Allow to cool completely.
2. **Prepare the Frosting:**
    - Whip the heavy cream with powdered sugar and vanilla until stiff peaks form.
3. **Assemble the Cake:**
    - Once the cakes are cooled, place one layer on a serving platter. Spread with whipped cream and top with cherries and chocolate shavings.
    - Place the second layer of cake on top. Frost with more whipped cream and garnish with remaining cherries and chocolate shavings.

Chocolate Banana Layer Cake

Ingredients

For the Cake:

- 1 ½ cups (190g) all-purpose flour
- 1 ½ tsp baking powder
- ½ tsp baking soda
- ¼ tsp salt
- 3 ripe bananas, mashed
- ½ cup (115g) unsalted butter, softened
- 1 cup (200g) granulated sugar
- 2 large eggs
- 1 tsp vanilla extract
- ½ cup (120ml) milk
- ¼ cup (60ml) sour cream

For the Chocolate Frosting:

- 1 ½ cups (180g) powdered sugar
- 1 cup (230g) unsalted butter, softened
- ¼ cup (60g) cocoa powder
- 2 tbsp milk
- 1 tsp vanilla extract

Instructions

1. **Prepare the Cake:**
    - Preheat the oven to 350°F (175°C). Grease and line two 9-inch (23cm) round cake pans.
    - In a bowl, whisk together flour, baking powder, baking soda, and salt.
    - In a separate bowl, beat together butter and sugar until fluffy. Add eggs one at a time, then stir in vanilla extract and mashed bananas.
    - Gradually add the dry ingredients, alternating with milk and sour cream. Mix until smooth.
    - Divide the batter between the pans and bake for 25-30 minutes or until a toothpick comes out clean. Allow to cool completely.
2. **Prepare the Chocolate Frosting:**
    - Beat together butter, powdered sugar, cocoa powder, milk, and vanilla until smooth and creamy.

3. **Assemble the Cake:**
    - Frost the cooled cakes with chocolate frosting.

Chocolate Cherry Almond Cake

Ingredients

For the Cake:

- 1 ¾ cups (220g) all-purpose flour
- 1 tsp baking powder
- ½ tsp baking soda
- ¼ tsp salt
- 1 cup (240ml) milk
- ½ cup (115g) unsalted butter, softened
- 1 ¼ cups (250g) granulated sugar
- 2 large eggs
- 1 tsp vanilla extract
- ½ tsp almond extract
- 1 cup (120g) maraschino cherries, chopped
- ½ cup (50g) slivered almonds

For the Frosting:

- 8 oz (225g) cream cheese, softened
- ½ cup (115g) unsalted butter, softened
- 3 cups (360g) powdered sugar
- 1 tsp almond extract
- 2 tbsp maraschino cherry juice

Instructions

1. **Prepare the Cake:**
   - Preheat the oven to 350°F (175°C). Grease and line two 9-inch (23cm) round cake pans.
   - In a bowl, whisk together flour, baking powder, baking soda, and salt.
   - In a separate bowl, beat together butter and sugar until fluffy. Add eggs one at a time, then stir in vanilla and almond extracts.
   - Gradually add the dry ingredients, alternating with milk. Fold in cherries and slivered almonds.
   - Divide the batter between the pans and bake for 25-30 minutes, or until a toothpick comes out clean. Allow to cool completely.
2. **Prepare the Frosting:**

- Beat together cream cheese, butter, powdered sugar, almond extract, and cherry juice until smooth and fluffy.
3. **Assemble the Cake:**
    - Frost the cooled cakes with the frosting.

Chocolate and Hazelnut Praline Cake

Ingredients

For the Cake:

- 2 cups (250g) all-purpose flour
- 1 ½ tsp baking powder
- ½ tsp baking soda
- ¼ tsp salt
- 1 cup (240ml) milk
- ½ cup (115g) unsalted butter, softened
- 1 ½ cups (300g) granulated sugar
- 3 large eggs
- 1 tsp vanilla extract
- 1 cup (120g) roasted hazelnuts, chopped

For the Frosting:

- 1 cup (230g) unsalted butter, softened
- 1 ½ cups (180g) powdered sugar
- 1/3 cup (80g) cocoa powder
- 2 tbsp heavy cream
- 1 tsp vanilla extract

For the Hazelnut Praline:

- 1 cup (200g) granulated sugar
- ½ cup (120g) roasted hazelnuts

Instructions

1. **Prepare the Cake:**
    - Preheat the oven to 350°F (175°C). Grease and line two 9-inch (23cm) round cake pans.
    - In a bowl, whisk together flour, baking powder, baking soda, and salt.
    - In a separate bowl, beat together butter and sugar until fluffy. Add eggs one at a time, then stir in vanilla extract.
    - Gradually add the dry ingredients, alternating with milk. Fold in chopped hazelnuts.

- Divide the batter between the pans and bake for 25-30 minutes or until a toothpick comes out clean. Allow to cool completely.
2. **Prepare the Frosting:**
    - Beat together butter, powdered sugar, cocoa powder, cream, and vanilla until smooth and fluffy.
3. **Prepare the Hazelnut Praline:**
    - Heat sugar in a pan until it melts into caramel. Stir in roasted hazelnuts and pour the mixture onto a baking sheet to cool. Once set, break into pieces.
4. **Assemble the Cake:**
    - Frost the cooled cakes with chocolate frosting and top with hazelnut praline pieces.

Chocolate Pumpkin Spice Cake

Ingredients

For the Cake:

- 1 ¾ cups (220g) all-purpose flour
- 1 tsp baking powder
- 1 tsp baking soda
- ½ tsp cinnamon
- ¼ tsp nutmeg
- ¼ tsp ground ginger
- ¼ tsp salt
- 1 cup (240ml) canned pumpkin
- ½ cup (115g) unsalted butter, softened
- 1 ½ cups (300g) granulated sugar
- 2 large eggs
- 1 tsp vanilla extract
- ½ cup (120ml) milk

For the Frosting:

- 8 oz (225g) cream cheese, softened
- ½ cup (115g) unsalted butter, softened
- 3 cups (360g) powdered sugar
- 1 tsp vanilla extract
- ½ tsp cinnamon

Instructions

1. **Prepare the Cake:**
    - Preheat the oven to 350°F (175°C). Grease and line two 9-inch (23cm) round cake pans.
    - In a bowl, whisk together flour, baking powder, baking soda, cinnamon, nutmeg, ginger, and salt.
    - In a separate bowl, beat together butter and sugar until fluffy. Add eggs one at a time, then stir in pumpkin and vanilla extract.
    - Gradually add the dry ingredients, alternating with milk, mixing until smooth.
    - Divide the batter between the pans and bake for 25-30 minutes, or until a toothpick comes out clean. Allow to cool completely.

2. **Prepare the Frosting:**
   - Beat together cream cheese, butter, powdered sugar, vanilla extract, and cinnamon until smooth and fluffy.
3. **Assemble the Cake:**
   - Frost the cooled cakes with cream cheese frosting.

Chocolate Tiramisu Layer Cake

Ingredients

For the Cake:

- 1 ¾ cups (220g) all-purpose flour
- 1 tsp baking powder
- ½ tsp baking soda
- ¼ tsp salt
- 1 cup (240ml) strong brewed coffee, cooled
- 1 cup (200g) granulated sugar
- ½ cup (115g) unsalted butter, softened
- 3 large eggs
- 1 tsp vanilla extract

For the Frosting:

- 1 cup (230g) mascarpone cheese
- 1 cup (240ml) heavy cream
- ½ cup (50g) powdered sugar
- 1 tbsp vanilla extract
- 2 tbsp coffee liqueur

Instructions

1. **Prepare the Cake:**
   - Preheat the oven to 350°F (175°C). Grease and line two 9-inch (23cm) round cake pans.
   - In a bowl, whisk together flour, baking powder, baking soda, and salt.
   - In a separate bowl, beat together butter and sugar until fluffy. Add eggs one at a time, then stir in vanilla extract and brewed coffee.
   - Gradually add the dry ingredients and mix until smooth.
   - Divide the batter between the pans and bake for 25-30 minutes, or until a toothpick comes out clean. Allow to cool completely.
2. **Prepare the Frosting:**
   - Beat together mascarpone cheese, heavy cream, powdered sugar, vanilla extract, and coffee liqueur until smooth and fluffy.
3. **Assemble the Cake:**
   - Frost the cooled cakes with tiramisu frosting.

Chocolate Lemon Layer Cake

Ingredients

For the Cake:

- 1 ½ cups (190g) all-purpose flour
- 1 ½ tsp baking powder
- ½ tsp baking soda
- ¼ tsp salt
- 1 cup (240ml) lemon juice
- ½ cup (115g) unsalted butter, softened
- 1 ¼ cups (250g) granulated sugar
- 2 large eggs
- 1 tsp vanilla extract
- Zest of 1 lemon

For the Frosting:

- 8 oz (225g) cream cheese, softened
- ½ cup (115g) unsalted butter, softened
- 3 cups (360g) powdered sugar
- 1 tsp vanilla extract
- 2 tbsp lemon zest

Instructions

1. **Prepare the Cake:**
    - Preheat the oven to 350°F (175°C). Grease and line two 9-inch (23cm) round cake pans.
    - In a bowl, whisk together flour, baking powder, baking soda, and salt.
    - In a separate bowl, beat together butter and sugar until fluffy. Add eggs one at a time, then stir in lemon juice and zest.
    - Gradually add the dry ingredients and mix until smooth.
    - Divide the batter between the pans and bake for 25-30 minutes, or until a toothpick comes out clean. Allow to cool completely.
2. **Prepare the Frosting:**
    - Beat together cream cheese, butter, powdered sugar, vanilla extract, and lemon zest until smooth and creamy.
3. **Assemble the Cake:**
    - Frost the cooled cakes with lemon cream cheese frosting.

Chocolate Mocha Ganache Cake

Ingredients

For the Cake:

- 1 ¾ cups (220g) all-purpose flour
- 1 tsp baking powder
- ½ tsp baking soda
- ¼ tsp salt
- ¾ cup (180ml) strong brewed coffee, cooled
- 1 cup (200g) granulated sugar
- ½ cup (115g) unsalted butter, softened
- 2 large eggs
- 1 tsp vanilla extract
- ¼ cup (60ml) milk
- 2 tbsp cocoa powder

For the Ganache:

- 8 oz (225g) dark chocolate, chopped
- ½ cup (120ml) heavy cream
- 1 tbsp coffee liqueur (optional)

Instructions

1. **Prepare the Cake:**
   - Preheat the oven to 350°F (175°C). Grease and line two 9-inch (23cm) round cake pans.
   - In a bowl, whisk together flour, baking powder, baking soda, salt, and cocoa powder.
   - In a separate bowl, beat together butter and sugar until fluffy. Add eggs one at a time, then stir in vanilla extract.
   - Gradually add the dry ingredients, alternating with coffee and milk, mixing until smooth.
   - Divide the batter between the pans and bake for 25-30 minutes, or until a toothpick comes out clean. Allow to cool completely.
2. **Prepare the Ganache:**
   - Heat heavy cream in a small saucepan over medium heat until it begins to simmer.

        - Pour over the chopped chocolate and stir until smooth. Add coffee liqueur (if using) and mix well.
3. **Assemble the Cake:**
        - Frost the cooled cakes with the ganache, letting it drip down the sides.

Chocolate and Macadamia Nut Cake

Ingredients

For the Cake:

- 1 ¾ cups (220g) all-purpose flour
- 1 tsp baking powder
- ½ tsp baking soda
- ¼ tsp salt
- 1 cup (200g) granulated sugar
- ½ cup (115g) unsalted butter, softened
- 2 large eggs
- 1 cup (240ml) buttermilk
- 1 tsp vanilla extract
- ½ cup (75g) macadamia nuts, chopped
- ¼ cup (60g) cocoa powder

For the Frosting:

- 8 oz (225g) cream cheese, softened
- 1 cup (115g) powdered sugar
- ½ cup (115g) unsalted butter, softened
- ¼ cup (60g) cocoa powder
- 1 tsp vanilla extract

Instructions

1. **Prepare the Cake:**
    - Preheat the oven to 350°F (175°C). Grease and line two 9-inch (23cm) round cake pans.
    - In a bowl, whisk together flour, baking powder, baking soda, salt, and cocoa powder.
    - In a separate bowl, beat together butter and sugar until fluffy. Add eggs one at a time, then stir in vanilla extract.
    - Gradually add the dry ingredients, alternating with buttermilk, mixing until smooth.
    - Fold in chopped macadamia nuts and divide the batter between the pans.
    - Bake for 25-30 minutes, or until a toothpick comes out clean. Allow to cool completely.
2. **Prepare the Frosting:**

- Beat together cream cheese, butter, powdered sugar, cocoa powder, and vanilla extract until smooth and creamy.
3. **Assemble the Cake:**
    - Frost the cooled cakes with the macadamia nut frosting.

Chocolate Toffee Cake

Ingredients

For the Cake:

- 1 ¾ cups (220g) all-purpose flour
- 1 tsp baking powder
- ½ tsp baking soda
- ¼ tsp salt
- 1 cup (200g) granulated sugar
- ½ cup (115g) unsalted butter, softened
- 2 large eggs
- ½ cup (120ml) milk
- ½ cup (100g) toffee bits
- ¼ cup (60g) cocoa powder

For the Frosting:

- 1 cup (240ml) heavy cream
- 8 oz (225g) dark chocolate, chopped
- 1 tsp vanilla extract
- ½ cup (100g) toffee bits

Instructions

1. **Prepare the Cake:**
    - Preheat the oven to 350°F (175°C). Grease and line two 9-inch (23cm) round cake pans.
    - In a bowl, whisk together flour, baking powder, baking soda, salt, and cocoa powder.
    - In a separate bowl, beat together butter and sugar until fluffy. Add eggs one at a time, then stir in milk.
    - Gradually add the dry ingredients and mix until smooth.
    - Fold in toffee bits and divide the batter between the pans.
    - Bake for 25-30 minutes, or until a toothpick comes out clean. Allow to cool completely.
2. **Prepare the Frosting:**
    - Heat heavy cream in a small saucepan over medium heat until it begins to simmer.
    - Pour over chopped chocolate and stir until smooth. Add vanilla extract.

    - Let the ganache cool to a thicker consistency, then frost the cake.
3. **Assemble the Cake:**
    - Frost the cooled cakes with toffee ganache and sprinkle with toffee bits.

Chocolate Almond Joy Cake

Ingredients

For the Cake:

- 1 ¾ cups (220g) all-purpose flour
- 1 tsp baking powder
- ½ tsp baking soda
- ¼ tsp salt
- 1 cup (200g) granulated sugar
- ½ cup (115g) unsalted butter, softened
- 2 large eggs
- 1 cup (240ml) buttermilk
- ½ cup (75g) shredded coconut
- ½ cup (75g) chopped almonds
- ¼ cup (60g) cocoa powder

For the Frosting:

- 8 oz (225g) cream cheese, softened
- 1 cup (115g) powdered sugar
- ½ cup (115g) unsalted butter, softened
- ¼ cup (60g) cocoa powder
- 1 tsp vanilla extract

Instructions

1. **Prepare the Cake:**
    - Preheat the oven to 350°F (175°C). Grease and line two 9-inch (23cm) round cake pans.
    - In a bowl, whisk together flour, baking powder, baking soda, salt, and cocoa powder.
    - In a separate bowl, beat together butter and sugar until fluffy. Add eggs one at a time, then stir in buttermilk.
    - Gradually add the dry ingredients and mix until smooth.
    - Fold in shredded coconut and chopped almonds. Divide the batter between the pans and bake for 25-30 minutes. Allow to cool.
2. **Prepare the Frosting:**
    - Beat together cream cheese, butter, powdered sugar, cocoa powder, and vanilla extract until smooth and creamy.

3. **Assemble the Cake:**
    - Frost the cooled cakes with frosting, and top with extra almonds and coconut.

Chocolate Cream Puff Cake

Ingredients

For the Cake:

- 1 ¾ cups (220g) all-purpose flour
- 1 tsp baking powder
- ½ tsp salt
- 1 cup (240ml) water
- ½ cup (115g) unsalted butter
- 4 large eggs
- ¼ cup (60g) cocoa powder
- 1 tsp vanilla extract

For the Frosting:

- 1 cup (240ml) heavy cream
- 2 tbsp powdered sugar
- 1 tsp vanilla extract

Instructions

1. **Prepare the Cake:**
    - Preheat the oven to 350°F (175°C). Grease and line a 9-inch (23cm) round cake pan.
    - In a saucepan, bring water and butter to a boil. Stir in flour, baking powder, salt, and cocoa powder, then remove from heat.
    - Add eggs one at a time, mixing thoroughly between each addition.
    - Stir in vanilla extract and bake for 25-30 minutes. Allow to cool.
2. **Prepare the Frosting:**
    - Beat together heavy cream, powdered sugar, and vanilla until soft peaks form.
3. **Assemble the Cake:**
    - Frost the cooled cake with whipped cream frosting.

Chocolate and Red Velvet Cake

Ingredients

For the Cake:

- 1 ¾ cups (220g) all-purpose flour
- 1 tsp baking powder
- ½ tsp baking soda
- ¼ tsp salt
- 1 cup (200g) granulated sugar
- ½ cup (115g) unsalted butter, softened
- 2 large eggs
- 1 tsp vanilla extract
- 1 tsp cocoa powder
- 1 cup (240ml) buttermilk
- 1 tbsp red food coloring

For the Frosting:

- 8 oz (225g) cream cheese, softened
- ½ cup (115g) unsalted butter, softened
- 3 cups (360g) powdered sugar
- 1 tsp vanilla extract

Instructions

1. **Prepare the Cake:**
    - Preheat the oven to 350°F (175°C). Grease and line two 9-inch (23cm) round cake pans.
    - In a bowl, whisk together flour, baking powder, baking soda, salt, and cocoa powder.
    - In a separate bowl, beat together butter and sugar until fluffy. Add eggs one at a time, then stir in vanilla and food coloring.
    - Gradually add the dry ingredients, alternating with buttermilk. Divide the batter between the pans and bake for 25-30 minutes.
2. **Prepare the Frosting:**
    - Beat together cream cheese, butter, powdered sugar, and vanilla extract until smooth.
3. **Assemble the Cake:**
    - Frost the cooled cakes with cream cheese frosting.

Chocolate Strawberry Shortcake Cake

Ingredients

For the Cake:

- 1 ¾ cups (220g) all-purpose flour
- 1 tsp baking powder
- ½ tsp baking soda
- ¼ tsp salt
- 1 cup (200g) granulated sugar
- ½ cup (115g) unsalted butter, softened
- 2 large eggs
- ½ cup (120ml) milk
- 1 tsp vanilla extract
- ¼ cup (60g) cocoa powder

For the Frosting:

- 1 cup (240ml) heavy cream
- 1 tbsp powdered sugar
- 1 tsp vanilla extract
- 1 ½ cups fresh strawberries, sliced

Instructions

1. **Prepare the Cake:**
    - Preheat the oven to 350°F (175°C). Grease and line two 9-inch (23cm) round cake pans.
    - In a bowl, whisk together flour, baking powder, baking soda, salt, and cocoa powder.
    - In a separate bowl, beat together butter and sugar until fluffy. Add eggs one at a time, then stir in vanilla and milk.
    - Gradually add the dry ingredients and mix until smooth. Divide the batter between the pans and bake for 25-30 minutes. Allow to cool.
2. **Prepare the Frosting:**
    - Beat heavy cream, powdered sugar, and vanilla until soft peaks form.
3. **Assemble the Cake:**
    - Frost the cooled cakes with whipped cream, top with strawberries.

Chocolate and Dulce de Leche Cake

Ingredients

For the Cake:

- 1 ¾ cups (220g) all-purpose flour
- 1 tsp baking powder
- ½ tsp baking soda
- ¼ tsp salt
- 1 cup (200g) granulated sugar
- ½ cup (115g) unsalted butter, softened
- 2 large eggs
- 1 tsp vanilla extract
- ¼ cup (60g) cocoa powder
- ½ cup (120ml) milk
- 1 cup (240ml) dulce de leche

For the Frosting:

- 8 oz (225g) cream cheese, softened
- 1 cup (115g) powdered sugar
- ¼ cup (60g) dulce de leche

Instructions

1. **Prepare the Cake:**
    - Preheat the oven to 350°F (175°C). Grease and line two 9-inch (23cm) round cake pans.
    - In a bowl, whisk together flour, baking powder, baking soda, salt, and cocoa powder.
    - In a separate bowl, beat together butter and sugar until fluffy. Add eggs one at a time, then stir in vanilla extract and milk.
    - Gradually add the dry ingredients and mix until smooth. Divide the batter between the pans and bake for 25-30 minutes. Let cool.
2. **Prepare the Frosting:**
    - Beat together cream cheese, powdered sugar, and dulce de leche until smooth.
3. **Assemble the Cake:**
    - Frost the cooled cakes with the dulce de leche frosting.

Chocolate Fudge and Pecan Cake

Ingredients

For the Cake:

- 1 ¾ cups (220g) all-purpose flour
- 1 tsp baking powder
- 1/2 tsp baking soda
- ¼ tsp salt
- 1 cup (200g) granulated sugar
- ½ cup (115g) unsalted butter, softened
- 2 large eggs
- 1 tsp vanilla extract
- 1 cup (240ml) milk
- 4 oz (115g) semi-sweet chocolate, melted
- 1 cup (120g) pecans, chopped

For the Frosting:

- 2 cups (240g) powdered sugar
- ½ cup (115g) unsalted butter, softened
- 2 tbsp cocoa powder
- 2-3 tbsp milk
- ½ cup (60g) chopped pecans for topping

Instructions

1. **Prepare the Cake:**
   - Preheat the oven to 350°F (175°C). Grease and line two 9-inch (23cm) round cake pans.
   - In a bowl, whisk together flour, baking powder, baking soda, and salt.
   - In a separate bowl, beat together butter and sugar until fluffy. Add eggs one at a time, then stir in vanilla extract and melted chocolate.
   - Gradually add the dry ingredients, alternating with milk, until smooth. Stir in chopped pecans.
   - Divide the batter between the pans and bake for 25-30 minutes. Let cool.
2. **Prepare the Frosting:**
   - Beat together powdered sugar, butter, cocoa powder, and milk until smooth and creamy.
3. **Assemble the Cake:**

- Frost the cooled cakes with the chocolate fudge frosting. Top with chopped pecans.

Chocolate and Bourbon Layer Cake

Ingredients

For the Cake:

- 1 ½ cups (190g) all-purpose flour
- 1 tsp baking powder
- 1 tsp baking soda
- ¼ tsp salt
- 1 cup (200g) granulated sugar
- ½ cup (115g) unsalted butter, softened
- 2 large eggs
- 1 tsp vanilla extract
- 1 cup (240ml) buttermilk
- ¼ cup (60ml) bourbon
- ¼ cup (60g) cocoa powder

For the Frosting:

- 1 ½ cups (360ml) heavy cream
- 2 cups (240g) powdered sugar
- 1 cup (240g) semi-sweet chocolate chips, melted
- 2 tbsp bourbon

Instructions

1. **Prepare the Cake:**
    - Preheat the oven to 350°F (175°C). Grease and line two 9-inch (23cm) round cake pans.
    - In a bowl, whisk together flour, baking powder, baking soda, salt, and cocoa powder.
    - In a separate bowl, beat together butter and sugar until light and fluffy. Add eggs one at a time, then stir in vanilla extract and bourbon.
    - Gradually add the dry ingredients, alternating with buttermilk, until smooth.
    - Divide the batter between the pans and bake for 25-30 minutes. Let cool.
2. **Prepare the Frosting:**
    - Beat heavy cream and powdered sugar until stiff peaks form. Gently fold in the melted chocolate and bourbon.
3. **Assemble the Cake:**
    - Frost the cooled cakes with the chocolate bourbon frosting.

Chocolate and Coconut Custard Cake

Ingredients

For the Cake:

- 1 ½ cups (190g) all-purpose flour
- 1 tsp baking powder
- ½ tsp baking soda
- ¼ tsp salt
- 1 cup (200g) granulated sugar
- ½ cup (115g) unsalted butter, softened
- 2 large eggs
- 1 tsp vanilla extract
- 1 cup (240ml) coconut milk
- 1 cup (100g) shredded coconut
- 2 tbsp cocoa powder

For the Custard:

- 1 cup (240ml) heavy cream
- 1 tbsp cornstarch
- 1 tbsp sugar
- ½ cup (120ml) coconut milk
- 2 egg yolks
- ¼ cup (60g) shredded coconut, toasted

Instructions

1. **Prepare the Cake:**
   - Preheat the oven to 350°F (175°C). Grease and line two 9-inch (23cm) round cake pans.
   - In a bowl, whisk together flour, baking powder, baking soda, salt, and cocoa powder.
   - In a separate bowl, beat together butter and sugar until fluffy. Add eggs one at a time, then stir in vanilla extract and coconut milk.
   - Gradually add the dry ingredients until smooth. Stir in shredded coconut.
   - Divide the batter between the pans and bake for 25-30 minutes. Let cool.
2. **Prepare the Custard:**
   - In a saucepan, whisk together heavy cream, coconut milk, sugar, and cornstarch. Cook over medium heat, stirring constantly, until thickened.

- In a separate bowl, whisk egg yolks, then slowly whisk in some of the hot cream mixture to temper the yolks. Gradually whisk the yolk mixture into the saucepan and cook for another 2 minutes. Remove from heat and cool.

3. **Assemble the Cake:**
    - Spread the custard between the layers of cake, topping with toasted coconut.

Chocolate Blueberry Truffle Cake

Ingredients

For the Cake:

- 1 ¾ cups (220g) all-purpose flour
- 1 tsp baking powder
- 1 tsp baking soda
- ¼ tsp salt
- 1 cup (200g) granulated sugar
- ½ cup (115g) unsalted butter, softened
- 2 large eggs
- 1 tsp vanilla extract
- 1 cup (240ml) milk
- ½ cup (120g) dark chocolate, melted
- 1 cup (150g) fresh blueberries

For the Frosting:

- 1 ½ cups (360ml) heavy cream
- 8 oz (225g) dark chocolate, chopped
- 1 cup (100g) blueberries for garnish

Instructions

1. **Prepare the Cake:**
    - Preheat the oven to 350°F (175°C). Grease and line two 9-inch (23cm) round cake pans.
    - In a bowl, whisk together flour, baking powder, baking soda, and salt.
    - In a separate bowl, beat together butter and sugar until light and fluffy. Add eggs one at a time, then stir in vanilla extract and melted chocolate.
    - Gradually add the dry ingredients, alternating with milk, until smooth. Gently fold in blueberries.
    - Divide the batter between the pans and bake for 25-30 minutes. Let cool.
2. **Prepare the Frosting:**
    - Heat heavy cream until just boiling. Pour over chopped chocolate and stir until smooth. Allow to cool to room temperature, then beat with a hand mixer until fluffy.
3. **Assemble the Cake:**

- Frost the cooled cakes with the chocolate frosting and top with fresh blueberries.

Chocolate Pistachio Cake

Ingredients

For the Cake:

- 1 ½ cups (190g) all-purpose flour
- 1 tsp baking powder
- ½ tsp baking soda
- ¼ tsp salt
- 1 cup (200g) granulated sugar
- ½ cup (115g) unsalted butter, softened
- 2 large eggs
- 1 tsp vanilla extract
- 1 cup (240ml) milk
- ½ cup (75g) chopped pistachios
- 2 tbsp cocoa powder

For the Frosting:

- 1 cup (240ml) heavy cream
- 2 cups (240g) powdered sugar
- 1 cup (150g) pistachio paste

Instructions

1. **Prepare the Cake:**
    - Preheat the oven to 350°F (175°C). Grease and line two 9-inch (23cm) round cake pans.
    - In a bowl, whisk together flour, baking powder, baking soda, salt, and cocoa powder.
    - In a separate bowl, beat together butter and sugar until fluffy. Add eggs one at a time, then stir in vanilla extract.
    - Gradually add the dry ingredients, alternating with milk, until smooth. Stir in chopped pistachios.
    - Divide the batter between the pans and bake for 25-30 minutes. Let cool.
2. **Prepare the Frosting:**
    - Beat together heavy cream, powdered sugar, and pistachio paste until smooth.
3. **Assemble the Cake:**
    - Frost the cooled cakes with pistachio frosting.

Chocolate Sour Cherry Cake

Ingredients

For the Cake:

- 1 ¾ cups (220g) all-purpose flour
- 1 tsp baking powder
- ½ tsp baking soda
- ¼ tsp salt
- 1 cup (200g) granulated sugar
- ½ cup (115g) unsalted butter, softened
- 2 large eggs
- 1 tsp vanilla extract
- 1 cup (240ml) milk
- 1 cup (150g) sour cherries, pitted and chopped
- 2 tbsp cocoa powder

For the Frosting:

- 1 ½ cups (360ml) heavy cream
- 8 oz (225g) semi-sweet chocolate, chopped
- ½ cup (75g) sour cherries for garnish

Instructions

1. **Prepare the Cake:**
    - Preheat the oven to 350°F (175°C). Grease and line two 9-inch (23cm) round cake pans.
    - In a bowl, whisk together flour, baking powder, baking soda, salt, and cocoa powder.
    - In a separate bowl, beat together butter and sugar until fluffy. Add eggs one at a time, then stir in vanilla extract.
    - Gradually add the dry ingredients, alternating with milk, until smooth. Stir in sour cherries.
    - Divide the batter between the pans and bake for 25-30 minutes. Let cool.
2. **Prepare the Frosting:**
    - Heat heavy cream until boiling. Pour over chopped chocolate and stir until smooth. Allow to cool to room temperature, then beat until fluffy.
3. **Assemble the Cake:**

- Frost the cooled cakes with the chocolate frosting and garnish with sour cherries.

www.ingramcontent.com/pod-product-compliance
Lightning Source LLC
LaVergne TN
LVHW081319060526
838201LV00055B/2366